# Unbeknownst To Me
## the hurt was in the healing

No part of this book may be reproduced or used in any form or by any means, electrical, mechanical, or otherwise, including, but not limited to, photocopy, recording, or any information storage and retrieval system, without prior written permission from the copyright owner, except in the case of brief quotations used in reviews.

Unbeknownst To Me the hurt was in the healing

Copyright 2021 by Marlo Sheppard All Rights Reserved

ISBN: 9798546200565

CreateSpace Independent Publishing Platform,
North Charleston, SC

## DEDICATION

Cameron, this is for you, My Baby!

I can't express how much gratitude I have for everything that you have done for me. You excepted nothing but my all; and all that came along with it. I love you always.

## ACKNOWLEDGEMENT

First and foremost, I give praise to my God! To all of my family and friends who have supported me, I will forever love you! Please know that the loyalty that you have given me is forever cherished.

## PREFACE

It's my time to soar in a season made specifically for me! I see things with my eyes that all can't. I must voice my feelings, to the fullest, in order to replenish what has been taken; and enrich what is healthy. Only I know how to adapt to my season. My growth is the intellect that is deep within me. My nourishment consists of the faith that guides me. The soil represents the life that flows throughout my veins. It is the source of the nutrients which are my thoughts. With the water, that represents the wisdom that is poured upon me, I grow…and grow…and grow. I am enriched with my support system. This method of fertilization is what will keep me strong. Without it, my life would encounter a delay from serving my purpose.

I have endured much in the time that I have spent on this earth. There have been exceptional, as well, as treacherous times, within my life. When my thoughts drift from the time I was a child up until the present, reality kicks in. I have been blessed in ways unimaginable. And I have encountered many who have crossed my path. When roads cross, the intersection determines which way the journey continues. Each and every one of these paths depicts a chapter in my life.

Twenty years ago, someone unexpectedly grabbed a hold of my spirit and didn't let go. This person is whom I refer to as an angel. I experienced a spiritual uplifting like never before. He delivered to me, a message of everlasting love, joy, and yes, peace. He revealed to me how the weeds, the difficult times, would be removed from my soil. Instead, new seeds (life's lessons) would be the replacement for the new harvest (blessings). As years passed, I noticed that he would quietly and carefully affirm information that only God and I knew. Again, this was a confirmation that he must have been sent from a higher being. When I think of him, benevolence is the word that best describes my angel. To this day, and on occasion, I still become so overwhelmed with tears of gratitude. And it reminds me of a true feeling of spiritual bliss and tranquility. When it all boils down to it, I must confess that I'm so happy. I feel those words with so much piety that I have no choice but to accept this blessing that was meant just for me.

Since accepting my true self, the perseverance within me has increased with a tremendous force. I can now share my testimony of overcoming sorrow and shedding tears of questioning…why. However, I can also share that the good days are plentiful, and my journey continues! My story is me. As a matter of fact, through all that I could bare, I stayed true to myself, and I continue to be me. No one can change the beauty within me. Nor can they change the very essence of my soul. My season is here! The affirmation has been put in place. My roots are spreading, and new life is in the midst. Life sustains the soul. Without a pure soul, there is no life.

My life depicts strengths as well as weaknesses; and embody all who have become a part of my existence. Some of my situations flourished and some did not. The growth consisted of the goodness that came out of various circumstances within my life. However, on the other hand, all that perished, are the ordeals that only did me harm. Therefore, I had to be removed from the tribulation so the virtue could continue to grow.

I'm forever craving to learn the wisdom that is required for me to become that fragrant bloom that is pleasing to all that cross my path. However, I also require continuous monitoring and care because I am not perfect. Believe it or not, thorns can hurt as well as protect. I can accept the constructive criticism that will help me with emotional, mental and physical stability. Should you see me become weak, water me with the knowledge that will give my nutrients (conceptions) a chance to accept, adapt and strengthen. Like an annual bloom, it may seemingly go away but the roots stay connected. And, before you know it, the bloom reappears. I like to think of this as replenishing my thoughts (assessing) and obtaining the necessary serenity that's needed within me. This will allow me to have the patience and comprehension of how to deal with life.

It would be foolish of me to think or say that I can accept the actions and thoughts of all. I must be conscientious of my words when relating my perspective on how I feel on various issues. It took me a long time to realize that my voice is what elevates me as an individual. If I have limitations placed on my words, what good can I really be? I have had the tendency to limit the use of my voice because I didn't wish to hurt the one that I was in communication with. But, while doing so, I wasn't aware that I was mostly hindering myself. The heart and mind are like a love affair. It feels good but you never know what the other has in store.

    Perseverance will assist one to flourish. For as far as the eye can see, the final product can be plentiful. This is the legacy that I strive to be; and leave for my family to be proud of. The roots are continuously expanding. This exhibits the connection with others. Positive influence can spread and will hopefully be a pathway to another's happiness. Find hope with a hug, fight for your faith, and turn your potential into your purpose.

    Nature (life) is what we make of it. Therefore, it's up to me to conquer my storms or make it through a drought. Storms are the ordeals coming at an individual from every which way. It sometimes comes with such fierceness, until one may feel helpless. Debris is blown from every angle. One can soon feel warn down, but suddenly the mood can switch. The wind eases, the rain is no longer pounding you, and there's a sense of relief. Behind the dark clouds there's a beam of sunshine. A rainbow appears, and you wonder what's on the other side. The mood becomes hopeful.

    Although there's a sensation of being overwhelmed, the ordeal eventually comes to a rest. At that moment you can refocus and realize what just took place. Storms are illustrations that flood the soul and brings the crops back to life. The drought is the idea that there's no progression in sight. Long suffering dries up the inner being. Moods of no replenishment, boggles the mind. Thirst becomes evident to all involved. There's a mission that needs to be accomplished. The thirst will be quenched once the agenda is acknowledged. Events in life can be unanticipated. But if there's enough fortification, any problem can be managed.

    It is my belief that everyone has a story and a purpose. Although, we tend to take it for granted that our individual problems don't matter to anyone else. This couldn't be further from the truth. As a matter of fact, your issue can indeed have an impact on another's life. Hearing one's knowledge may aspire another to abide.

    Sometimes society tends to focus on the bad outweighing the good. Lucky for us, the good certainly does exist. Whenever possible, it is up to us to keep our lives in order. If we manage to do so, there's a greater chance of spreading the joy and love that is needed to survive. Please know that your days will not always be sunny. You will have some gray days, as well. But keep your hearts and souls open to the unforeseen because this is where your blessings creep in. Now, with all that has been laid out before you…I ask…how will you flourish the essence of your soul?

## CHAPTER ONE
### Cameo of Me

Growing up, I never thought of myself as anyone special. But I knew that I wanted to be friendly and loving to everyone. My mama (Murline) and grandmama (Arie) taught me to know God and never lose faith. We didn't have much money, but we had a lot of love, nurturing, pride and discipline in our home.

I am my mother's third child; and remained the baby until ten years later when she birthed my baby sister. For the first three years of my life, I lived mostly with my god-family. My mama agreed to allow me to stay with my god-family during the week so that she would not have to worry about a babysitter while she went to work.

I was blessed that I had not only my mother, but grandparents and a god-family who loved me dearly. I was given a lot of stability as a result of having so much support. My innocence was guarded at all costs by my family. They reminded me on how vulnerable, quiet, and kind-hearted I was even as a child. As I grew older, I faced many challenges with maintaining the innocence within me. However, I also learned to be strong and resilient despite the challenge.

## CHAPTER TWO
### The Victory Within

As a child I can only remember having one fight with a boy on the school bus for pulling my hair. I was so damn scared after I confronted him for what seemed like the whole ride to school. We attended Burbank School which was a distance from where we lived. Detroit Public Schools were making attempts to do more integration. So, many of the black students had been bussed from our neighborhood, to other areas where many white families lived. Anyway, after asking him to stop pulling my hair, he decided that he would push me down in the seat; and then all hell broke loose. I kicked and swung my arms like I had lost my mind! After the other kids and driver realized what happened, everyone was in disbelief. My bus driver stopped the bus and ran to the back where we were fighting. The driver bent over laughing so hard, because she knew that fighting was not a part of my character, and that the boy that I was fighting had to be the reason for the altercation. Being that I got the most swings and he got the bulk of scratches, I was pumped with pride that I beat up a boy for pulling my hair. The fact is, he never even hit me; he only wanted to wrestle me down. As we unloaded the bus, my self-empowered soul, opened my mouth and yelled "I bet you wont mess with me again". This was one of my first lessons about being treated with respect. My mother always stressed that I should never allow anyone to treat me bad, and to always take up for myself.  Up until that point, I only needed to prove this with my brother who picked on me every day, but who was always the protector.  I've always wondered if my brother was on the bus that day if things would have been different. After all, my brother made it known to everyone that he was my big brother as a means to keep me safe.  If he didn't, there was going to be a problem when he got home to my mama.

    I've fought with myself many times because throughout my life, I had allowed my loyalty to disregard the lack of respect from others.  As a result, I've been hurt emotionally and struggled with making decisions that my heart didn't necessarily agree with. But my mind and common sense knew what was required.  I'm a firm believer in learning from past mistakes.  And although we don't like it, sometimes we must be brave enough to also hold ourselves accountable for our actions; because ultimately, that is where you get an opportunity to fight with integrity and grow from the experience.

## CHAPTER THREE
### Mending The Pieces

When my mama was a little girl, she and her brother were separated. She lived with her mama in Mississippi and my uncle was taken to live with their father who moved away to St. Louis. Although they had the same father, my mother hated the fact that she felt she was left behind, and didn't feel wanted by their father. She suffered with that pain for years, even throughout adulthood. I can only remember meeting my biological grandfather once in my life which was during my uncle's funeral. I recall meeting this light-skinned man who seemed so kind. It was amazing to me that my uncle was my grandmother's beautiful dark brown complexion and had her facial features; and my mother looked like my grandfather.

I think that my mother's hurt was turned into a mode of protection for her. She taught me, my sisters and brother to always take care of each other and don't let nobody put their hands on us. In other words, always be ready to help one another. She didn't feel like she had that growing up. But she learned to love her big family of cousins who treated her like a sister and protected her just the same.

When my grandmama married her husband Alfred, my mother bonded with him; and you would have never known that he wasn't her biological father. Mama loved him so much, and he would give her the world if he could. When she was in grade school, she began to write the last name of Franklin on her schoolwork which was Alfred's last name. Believe it or not, my mama's birth certificate had listed her last name as Johnikin which is our family's generational name. Well, she was never questioned, and she kept the last name of Franklin until her death. Not only did she carry on the Franklin name, but all four of her children were named after his legacy as well. I know my granddaddy, Alfred, would be proud. The Franklin family has grown tremendously.

    Like my mother, I also lived most of my years away from my father, but we have a loving relationship. I saw him often before our move from Memphis, in the summer, and talk to him often. From his marriage I also have two additional brothers. My mother would show me photos of my brothers when I was little so I could feel some type of connection to them. I constantly thought of one day meeting them. When I became an adult, I got a call from my father letting me know that my brother was getting married and wanted me to attend the wedding. I was elated and could not wait to finally meet my brothers, after so many years had passed. I finally felt that the missing piece in my life was found.

    I am my mama's child. So, when we made up our mind to do something…it was a done deal. I think she is the reason why I love so hard, take loyalty to another level, and don't waste a lot of time asking for help. Sometimes, I felt that was more of a curse to resist asking for help. But I also soon learned that you can ask for help only so many times before you must do things for yourself. I feel that when you work to get things done yourself, you tend to appreciate the process more. I was never good at feeling either dismissed, not appreciated, or important enough. I assume that this is where most of my resilience emerges from. Even when I felt hurt or not treated the best, I would always manage to find a way out of no way.

    I try to learn from my hardships and turn them into strengths. I've always tried to minimize the thought of not being able to overcome. Strength is in all of us. We just need to find a way to realize what we have, what needs to be gotten rid of, and how to make "it" (the positive outcome) happen. Think of it this way. If you're being chased by a dog and you fall, you are going to catch your breath, get the hell up, and continue to run until you get to a safe space. Life is the same way. It's not meant to be easy, but there is satisfaction that can be gained. I know what you may be thinking…better said than done. But it is attainable. Always focus on your strengths. I don't care how small you think it may be. It's the combination of those small strengths that will build you up. It's in all of us.

## CHAPTER FOUR
### I Am Who I Am

One day as I was playing with my brother, my mama asked me to come to her. She just kind of stared at me and didn't say anything for what seemed like the longest time. She had one of those looks of fear but trying her hardest not to show that fear to me. I guess after she realized what she was looking at, she began to ask me questions. She inquired if my face hurt and did it feel funny. I answered "no ma'am". Then she took me to the mirror and asked me to look at myself. My face had drooped really bad on one side of my face. Mama didn't play any games when it came to her kids. Before I knew it, we were on the city bus going to Children's Hospital in Detroit Medical Center.

I was diagnosed with Bell's Palsy, which was unfamiliar to us. We were soon educated on the diagnosis and I was tested as needed. The doctor asked me if the kids at school teased me; and I answered yes. He told me that no matter what, to remember that I was pretty; and the next time the kids teased me; to lick my tongue out at them. That made me smile and gave me a since of acceptance. After many visits, and participating in a medical study program, the medications began to work. My facial muscles eventually got stronger, and the drooping appearance was no longer visible. During this time in my life, I was around six years of age. And I can remember doing something that a child my age should not have had to even think about. I decided at that time, that a person had to like me for me. If they couldn't do that for me, I didn't want to be their friend or have anything to do with them. To this day, I still hold that time in my life close at heart, and develop from it every day.

## CHAPTER FIVE
### Move Over Heartache

There were two big moves that we made that impacted my life greatly. The first one was when we moved from Memphis to Detroit, when I was about four or five years old. I missed my god family a lot. For a few years, I would spend summers with them. But that eventually stopped. I later found out that my godmother couldn't bare the thought of having to see me leave, whenever my mother decided to take me back home to Detroit. So, she became upset and asked my mother to not send me back to Memphis. My mother never shared that story with me. I'm sure she was only protecting my feelings. However, I am so grateful that I did get to see my godparents again after I became an adult. Although my god mother was ill & living with dementia, she remembered me. My last visit with her was while she was hospitalized. God mama held my hand and smiled with as much strength as she could give. I knew at that moment that she never stopped loving me. Shortly after that visit, my godmother passed away.

Just as I was ending my first year at Joy Middle School my mother decided it was time to move this time to California. All I could focus on was how bad that idea was, and I was totally against having to move. My brother of course was willing and ready for

"Cali". He kept constantly reminding me that we would have no snow, it will always be sunny and hot, we will be able to go to the beach, and he was fascinated by the thought of seeing palm trees. I was so mad at him that I couldn't see straight! He was supposed to be on my side. It didn't matter to me though. I was determined that I was not going. The sooner it came time for us to leave, the more distant my attitude became. My mother noticed my behavior and asked me what was wrong. I told her that I didn't want to go and begged her to let me stay with my grandparents to finish the next school year at Joy. She eventually gave in but warned me that she would be back in the summer to take me to California. I was so happy to know that I didn't have to go. That whole year was good. I didn't have my brother harassing the hell out of me, I was doing good in school as always, and I was finally in beginner's band!

But just as the summer began the following year, my mother kept her word, and was coming to move me out to California. Let me tell you, I was so hurt and in disbelief. I just knew she would forget about it, and I would continue to stay with my grandparents. Please, allow me to remind you, my mama didn't play games when it came to her children. And she would always let us know "I meant what I said". All that I'm going to say is, that was the longest ride to California ever.

After we arrived in California, I was so sad and angry. I think it was more of depression, and I isolated myself. I stayed in my room and read books all day. I didn't want to meet any friends. The only time I came out of my room was to go to the bathroom or eat. After practically the whole summer passing me by, my mama put her foot down. She came in my room; forced me to go outside to meet some friends and I had better be able to tell her their names when I came in. I was mad as hell! But I knew one thing. I had better get my mad ass outside and meet some friends. My mama didn't play talking back to her by no means. I can't ever recall getting a "whipping" from her and wasn't planning on it either. For those that don't know what a "whipping" is. That is a black mama's way of using her best friend, also known as a belt, to help her make her point while saying a word with every lick!! I may have been mad, but I wasn't crazy enough to try her patience.

    I eventually met many friends and still have relationships with them to this day. I must admit that although the moves were hurtful to me, I am thankful that my mama taught me the lesson of not being able to always have things go my way. I learned that there will be plenty of times that I will not be able to control what happens in life. However, it's the hope of making the adjustment and coping in positive ways that we should be focused on. When I felt like I was alone with my wants, I ultimately had support that I didn't even recognize, such as my big head brother, mama and eventually new friends.

## CHAPTER SIX
### It's About to Get Real

So, let's fast forward a few years to my teens. By this time, I am well adjusted to the "Cali" life. I'm starting to notice boys but one in particular at the age of thirteen. His name was Hassan and was a great example of a first-time boyfriend who was kind and respectful to me. As a matter of fact, he was the template of how I wanted to be treated by a guy. However, he was afraid of my mama. Initially when they met, she scared the heck out of him and she must have asked him a thousand questions. After his interrogation, he proved that he was an ok guy to my mama. She gave him a lecture of what was expected of him and told him not to mess it up. I hadn't even experienced my first kiss until then; and I was still learning the ropes about boys. Don't get me wrong, mama schooled me on the dos and don'ts but of course I had to learn the hard way.

Eventually, at the age of fifteen I became pregnant and birthed a stillborn son. This was my first time having the experience of losing a close family member, not to mention, my own baby. That was a difficult time for me. I felt a sadness that I had never felt before. I cried all the time and just wanted to give up on everything. It took me a while to completely grieve but with the help of family and friends I made it through. After a few more years had passed, I birthed our second son Taji. I was thankful to God for my healthy baby, and I was determined to prove that not all teens were bad moms.

As I was forced to mature, I learned what it meant to be a hard worker and care for my son. At the same time, I attended school and worked. Again, I was determined to prove that I could make it as a teen mom and be proud about doing it. As I rode the city bus one day with my baby strapped to me in his carrier, I felt the stares from a woman sitting near me. Although I was mad at the blatant disrespect she showed towards me with her mean expressions, I looked at her with a smile and asked how she was doing. It caught her off guard. She proceeded to ask personal questions and I made sure I answered every one of her questions, staring directly in her eyes with respect and pride.

My mama always taught me to be proud of who I am no matter what. And on that day riding the bus I could have lit it on fire from the gleam that I felt, and how I intentionally presented myself with grace. While smiling until I felt like my face was about to crack, I remembered saying to myself "I'm doing this to show people like you lady". By the time the woman and I departed ways, she ended up being the nicest person ever & congratulated me on doing such a good job with caring for me and my baby. I have never shied away from my faults, yet I learned to seek gratification with my accomplishments.

When our son turned four, Hassan passed away from injuries that he sustained from a fight. And, coincidently on the same night as his fight, I dreamed of Hassan banging on a clear glass partition with his fist, trying to break it, to get to me. Unfortunately, he couldn't get through the glass. The following morning his mom called me while I was at work, to let me know that Hassan had passed away. When he died it was around the same time as my dream. I felt totally numb and couldn't function at work. My boss gave me the rest of the day off to be with my son. For many years after losing Hassan, it was pretty much just me and our son. Taji & I moved to San Diego to make a better life with new opportunities a year or so before Hassan's death. I always promised Hassan that I would take good care of our son no matter what. And that is what I did.

Years later, I met the man that eventually would become my husband. He was enlisted in the Marines and stationed at Camp Pendelton Marine Base in Oceanside, California. At first it was great. He and my son became close, and I felt that he was good for us. He was disciplined, fun, and attentive. However, he eventually moved back home to Detroit shortly after we gave birth to our first daughter Imani.

In time, my two children and I also moved back to Detroit. I knew that if things didn't work out with me and him, that I had my grandparents nearby. We got married in December of 1995. We had a second daughter Monai who was also a healthy baby. But as our family grew bigger, my marriage became more troubled, unhealthy & violent. Don't get me wrong, we had good times too. But the rough times started to become increasingly overwhelming. My husband and I tried hard to make it work but I knew that God saw different for me. The additional hurt and trauma was so new to my life. Yet, all that I could concentrate on was that I had to make my marriage work; and did what I had to do to care for my three babies, so I stayed and suffered.

For years, I lived with the guilt of not leaving, fear of not having stability for my children, not having my children raised in a two-parent home, lack of finances to live on my own, & giving up on my marriage. And wouldn't luck have it. During all the making up between the unrest, I again became pregnant. Mama always said I was her most fertile child and by this point, no one could tell me any different.

With all of the stress that I was going through, I went into early labor when I reached five months of pregnancy. Our son was born but was not strong due to his premature birth. As a matter of fact, both my baby and I remained inpatient, but the baby was transferred to Children's Hospital for intensive care. My doctor gave me a clearance to go see my baby, but I had to return to Hutzel Hospital after the visit. I had a c-section and was not healed enough to be discharged. I wasn't told by my husband until we got to Children's that our baby was dying. I looked at him and asked him why would he say something like that and was not prepared for what was to follow. My baby only lived for two days. I was able to see him and rub his hand while he laid in his incubator before he passed. He was hooked up to so many monitors. My focus was on him though. He was so beautiful with soft skin and jet black, silky hair. I will never forget how he looked at me, with him being so tiny. It was if he was telling me that he was going to be ok no matter what. I knew in my heart that it wouldn't be long before he and God would meet.

When I got the news that my baby died, I was alone in my hospital room & I cried with no remorse. On that day, the nurses at Hutzel Hospital were my saving grace. They sat, prayed, and hugged me with purpose. It felt as if God himself, meticulously picked out each one for the task at hand. I was even put in a private room so I wouldn't be triggered or further traumatized by being in a room with another new mom loving her baby. I will never forget those nurses for as long as I live. Losing my baby was the most inconceivable thing I felt I had to go through. If you remember, I had already lost one son and now another. This time the trauma felt ten times worse. After I was discharged and we drove home from the hospital, I could literally feel my whole body just doing its own thing. It felt as if every nerve in my body went haywire. As we pulled into our driveway, I remember my mother-in-law asking my husband, "what's wrong with her"? They didn't know what to do. Our neighbors walked to our truck to welcome me home with love, but all I remember is seeing many of their speechless faces filled with tears. My husband had to carry me into the house because I could not gain control of my body. To this day I know in my heart that I was suffering from a nervous breakdown.

After months of healing physically and spiritually, I reminisce about getting out of my chair one day, and rapidly started pacing the hall praying. I was begging God to help me to move forward. I felt so stuck; and I was beginning to feel afraid due to not knowing what was going to happen next, if I didn't beat that feeling of depression, grief, PTSD, and trauma that I was going through.

Like clockwork, I began to heal and get stronger as the days and weeks followed. If I don't know anything else, the God that I serve has never failed me. I knew that I didn't always do what was right, but at least I tried, and feel that God takes that into consideration. I am so grateful for that. No one is perfect. So, there are most likely going to be some faults. My faith is what has sustained me, and I knew that if I didn't have anything else…I had faith.

A shove here and there and words that pierced my soul as he yelled in rage at indescribable measure. No mercy within these walls; I better be ready for whatever come what may. Deep wounds don't heal…quick enough that is.

## CHAPTER SEVEN
### Time For a Change…the Turning Point

For a while the anger and rage within my home subsided. I just knew that with all that we had been through, that we would be good from that point. I guess that was wishful thinking. Gradually, the yelling resumed, and things were back to not knowing if the day was going to be a good day or a bad one.

One day I went to the grocery store to get food for the house. I returned to my husband yelling, "Where have you been…what took you so long"? My brother who was visiting, and I had a look of shock on our faces as I tried to explain that I had only been to the store. He had so much control over what I did and always seemed to time me whenever I left the house. Before I knew it, he went to one of the other rooms and got one of his guns. He was so mad that he was shaking and crying with rage. "You don't even love me. I will kill all of us". My brother was begging me to tell him that I loved him with the hope of de-escalating the situation. I stood up with conviction and didn't speak one mumbling word after looking at my brother to acknowledge him. I wasn't afraid anymore. And all that I could think was if he is going to do this, he'd better do it right. The empathy that encouraged his behavior, I would no longer contribute to. I'd be damned if he got another I love you out of me, after acting an ass, and treating me so bad. I was determined not to give him that power over me anymore. My brother eventually got him to calm down. Honestly, I cannot tell you what was going through my husband's head or what he was dealing with to make him go to such extreme. I knew that I could no longer trust him and if he knew any better, he'd better not trust me. I was tired and knew deep in my heart that one of us was going to get hurt if a change didn't come quick. I made up my mind that I would gradually start planning on leaving with all three of my children with me. The first thing I could think of was to make sure no more babies came, so I went to visit my doctor to get on birth control. I guess God wanted to play this scene out a little differently. Instead of birth control, I came home with a positive pregnancy test. Damn.

## Unbeknownst To Me

> People just don't know what I'm about
> They haven't seen what's there behind my smile
> There's so much more of me I'm showing now
> These are the pieces of me
> When it looks like I'm up, sometimes I'm down
> I'm alone even with people all around
> But that don't change the happiness I found
> These are the pieces of me

"Pieces of Me" by Ledisi Young, Claude Kelly and Chuck Harmony.

## CHAPTER EIGHT
Cameron's Journey

On May 24, 2000, to my surprise, I discovered that I was pregnant. Regardless of what I had been through, I knew on that day that God blessed me with another son. My spirit eventually soared from anticipation and excitement. I honestly felt that all that I had been going through was not in vain. God was giving me another chance to be blessed with another angel. This angel would be able to stay on earth with us and teach what the true meaning of love, patience, and understanding was all about. If I had to sum it all up in one word, it would of course be "faith".

As the months passed by, I'd began to look forward to going to my appointments to hear my baby's heartbeat. On June 20, 2000, I had my first ultrasound and too our amazement, the picture looked like an angel with a halo over his head. I didn't want to confirm the sex of the baby. So, every time I had an ultrasound, I declined on getting the answer to the question "Do you want to know what the baby is"?

On August 8, 2000, it was decided that I would get a cerclage as a precaution for preterm labor. I had a tilted cervix which made me high risk. The procedure was done on August 15, 2000. While in the pe-operative area my husband and I had a lot to talk about. Up until the eighth month, we basically had no worries.

November 21, 2000, during my ultrasound, I finally broke down and accepted confirmation that the baby was definitely a boy! "Thank you, Jesus" was my verbal reaction.

As the ultrasound exam continued, it was discovered that the baby had a medical condition referred to as an absent corpus collosum, on the right side of his head. Although this concerned the doctors the most, a calm spirit inside of me had told me that my baby was going to be just fine; just keep your "faith", and that is what I did. On January 3, 2001, I was thirty-six weeks, and the cerclage was removed which meant that if I went into labor that the chances of complication would be minimal.

My water broke on January 5, 2001, at 1:30am! My husband was at work but met me at Hutzel Hospital. I drove myself but had my little sister ride with me after convincing him on the phone that I would be ok.

At 8:01am, Cameron entered the outside world by c-section. He was born to one of my favorite gospel songs "Open Up My Heart" by Yolanda Adams. That song represented so much meaning and helped me to get through some rough moments. My husband had tears of joy and a sense of accomplishment. I felt as if the angelic spirit of Cameron's big brother had been holding his hand through it all, and was with him the whole way.

The pediatric team examined Cameron and found that he had a hematoma with bleeding on the right side, between his skull and the tissue that covers the brain, as well as being anemic, jaundiced, and unable to reproduce his red blood cells which led to breathing difficulties because of lack of oxygen. He had to be put on a ventilator to help him to breath and was given a blood transfusion.

On January 7, 2001, his godparents and I went to Cameron's bedside in Hutzel's NICU to pray for him. Shortly after, he was given another blood transfusion. The love, care and support he was given was a confirmation of what the power of prayer could do because the days that followed were miraculous.

The next day Cameron was transported to Children's Hospital for more intensive treatment. As the days passed by, he was no longer anemic, taken off of oxygen, and then his jaundice was gone. He had tubes and tubes of blood that was drawn to be tested. The doctors could not figure out why all of his tests were coming up negative, even though he had this mysterious clot and bleed in his head. A couple of the doctors would hint in so many words that God was working! We were told that the clot should dissolve on its own in time, but that we would have to take him in for follow up appointments.

We sat with Cameron everyday from January 9, 2001, through January 21, 2001. I had staples from the c-section but refused to let a day go by without him hearing my voice and feeling my touch. Cameron was discharged from Children's Hospital on January 21, 2001. We were so excited to get him home. He was officially the new boss of the house!

As we began to take Cameron for his follow up appointments the news grew increasingly troublesome. Initially, we were told by doctors that he would not be expected to survive beyond six months of age and to prepare. After reaching six months of age, we were then given a one-year survival rate. Once he turned one year old, I was then asked by the doctor "Mrs. Sheppard, what are you doing?" My response was simply "loving him."

## CAM'S LULLABY

Don't you, don't you cry my little baby
Don't you, don't you cry my little baby
Mommy is right here
Gonna' keep you safe and near
So, don't you don't you cry my little baby

Don't you, don't you cry my little baby
Don't you, don't you cry my little baby
Poppy loves you through and through
He will turn your grey skies, blue
So, don't you don't you cry my little baby

Don't you, don't you cry my little baby
Don't you, don't you cry my little baby
Jesus will provide
Never fear and never hide
So, don't you don't you cry my little baby

God grant me the serenity

to accept the things I cannot change,

Courage to change the

things I can,

And the wisdom to know

The difference.


"The Serenity Prayer" by Reinhold Niebuhr

## CHAPTER NINE
### Unwavering Bonds of Sibling Love – The Pact

Taji

The big brother who loves his brother unconditionally. Whenever Taji came home from hanging out with his friends, he made it his business to find Cameron and sit with him. Many times, it would just be the two of them smiling and laughing with one another. Taji never had a problem with taking care of Cam no matter where we were. He would change his diaper in the back of the church, take him to outings, and just be the best big brother he knew how to be. I continue to be proud of the relationship and bond that they shared.

Imani

The nurturing big sister is how I would describe her. Always ready to feed, clean, and just put 110% into caring for her brother. She didn't tolerate anyone feeling pity either. She will tell you in a minute "My brother is good"! And practically dared anyone to say otherwise after stating it. In other words, he had so much love and support that he didn't have time not to feel loved and supported, even when he wasn't feeling physically strong. And we (my children and I) wasn't having any pity parties between us as his support. As a matter a fact, it brought us so much closer.

## Monai

This sister is what I would consider the fun and bold sister. Monai was always the sister that would take chances on doing things with Cameron. When she was around six years old, she got fed up with me for telling her to wait, when it came to her and Imani wanting to share time with him. Monai actually strategized a plan to steal my baby out the living room one day. They took him to their room, secured him in his baby seat and sat on both sides as if they were his guarded security team! That was when I realized that they had learned more than enough and was willing and able to care for their brother just as much as I could.

*******************************

There hasn't been a day that I don't remember all three of my older children being by Cameron's side even when he was hospitalized. Mostly, Taji. It didn't matter what time of day it was. He usually had one of the Partner Passes given to parents and care givers of patients at Children's Hospital. The passes allowed us to visit at any time of the day, and the ability to stay overnight. There have been many times of the wee hours that Taji would walk through Cameron's hospital room door after getting off work at two o'clock in the morning. This proved to me and others, time and time again, of how much he was dedicated to his baby brother.  The staff was always pleased to see Taji who would consistently ask questions about his baby brother's treatment.  Sometimes I would just sit and let him ask all of the questions because I always knew that Taji was going to ask until he couldn't ask anymore.  In other words, the nurses and doctors had better make it clear enough for him to understand everything relating to Cameron's medical treatment.  I will always admire that about Taji.

  Imani and Monai would make it to the hospital for visits as well but were more time restricted due to caring for their own children.  Needless to say, that did not stop them from calling hourly and video chatting just to talk and laugh with Cameron.  Even when Cameron wasn't feeling his best, it was a relief for them to at least see his face.

  Cameron's sisters and brother have been instrumental with caring for him all of his life.  On the first day we brought him home from the hospital, we agreed that we would all help care for, and love him no matter what.  Now, keep in mind that they were about fourteen, seven and five years old at that time.  Taji, Imani & Monai took that promise to heart.  Not only did they love him, but also attended his needs by learning how to give his medication, tube feeds, baths, repositioning and everything in between.  They've always protected him with their all and loved him unconditionally.  Even with their own growing pains and life lessons, they had always put Cameron first.  I am blessed to be able to express that.

  My children have taught me that reciprocity of love is real.  They have had my back in ways I can't even explain, and when I least expected it. There have been many days that I needed time to relax to practice a little self-care; and they would be ready and willing to give me that time to do so. For instance, I would take a "Me Day" for a few hours; they would have dinner cooked; or simply sit with Cameron and allow me a nap. They even took turns getting Cam off of his school bus and caring for him after school, made sure their chores were done, and allowed me time to study while earning both of my college degrees. Some of the simplest things that meant so much. God has truly blessed Cameron with great siblings, and I would not trade them for anything in this world. Don't get me wrong, my children can be a hot mess sometimes LOL! But overall, they are my most cherished.

## CHAPTER TEN
### His Strength…My Guide

    As Cameron grew, so did his medical challenges. There were plenty of nights that I constantly asked God if I was doing absolutely all that I could to keep him safe, happy, and living. Seemingly, each time I asked that question it was Cameron who would give me the answer. He has been on life support at least four times throughout his life. One of those moments was in November 2016. He was only fifteen years old. Imagine being in the emergency room. Suddenly, over a loudspeaker you hear "code blue, trauma" and his bed number being yelled. Suddenly all you see are doctors, nurses, and staff running from every which way, back and forth, trying to save your child's life as you watch helplessly. It was terrifying. My heart was racing, face full of tears, shaking uncontrollably from nerves, and not being able to even touch him because I would only be in the way of his life being saved. That is a hard thing for a mother to eyewitness.

    My life changed as of that day, and I didn't see things as I did before. From that moment I really felt that I had no time to waste and that every beat of my heart would be dedicated to my son. Yes, I became more and more anxious as the years have come and gone. But that comes along with all the different emotions, ups and downs, anxiety, repetitious grief, depression, feelings of loneliness, and simply put…the uncertainties that came along with loving my baby son. And guess what? I would not dare change a damn thing.

Cameron showed me what it meant to live whole-heartedly, and in every aspect of doing so. Here he was, fighting to live with multiple disabilities and medical issues but still figuring out how to carry on despite the challenge. He showed me how to conquer when I least expected a victory. Not letting the quicksand of life pull me in; but instead, scratch, kick and pull myself out of life's trenches.

He has never spoken a word in all his twenty years of living. I take that back, there was one time that I could have sworn that I heard him say mama when he was about three years old. I will never forget the joy I felt after hearing it! Although I never heard him say it again, I cherished that one time and will live with the joy that he brought to me that day. He eventually dealt with issues with his esophagus which I think had a lot to do with him not speaking. Even though he could not verbally express himself, besides using certain sounds; expressions and gestures, I promise that once you got to know him, he could seemingly share long conversations with you. Cameron was just that relatable. He knew when to smile, listen quietly, laugh with a gut burst and sometimes give you the stink eye. No matter what, I felt that he always understood me and would be there to listen to my thoughts and secrets as a best friend would. I miss that feeling the most. He always knew how to respond to me at the most appropriate time.

Another great trait that he influenced in me was the ability to forgive in order to progress. He taught me that patience is key to forgiveness. In order for me to move forward with my dreams; as well as care for me and my children, I had to slow myself down so that I could focus on what my desires were. I found that if I concentrated on the hurt, that my mind would race and would lead to anger and resentment. However, when I lead the way with serenity, patience and forgiveness, it allowed the process to move more consistently and steady.

    We must be willing to forgive ourselves as well as others. I put a lot of pressure on myself in the past years and had no ability to control the process. Know that it is ok to recognize your weaknesses. When I began to relate to my faults, I was then able to reassess to determine how to resolve in a more attainable manner. Sometimes I had these huge & magnificent ideas, but they never manifested because I wasn't prepared due to not having a proper plan that worked specifically for me.

    It's my prayer, that I can touch at least one other mother who may have had similar life experiences as mine. Know that you are not alone, and that there are plenty of other mothers who are going through life the same way, if not worse. The key is knowing when to acknowledge; do not be afraid to ask for support; and be ready to excel with the potential to be as great as you want to be. Try to focus on your strengths which will give you encouragement. Take care of yourself. If you are not good, how will you be able to take care of those babies? Be willing to take risks, only if safe to do so. If not, make a plan that will get you to a safe space with supportive folks around you. It's ok to acknowledge your needs and weaknesses. Remember, you are human. As many have stated, it takes a village...

I pray you are finding a peace of mind, motivation to move you and blessings to sustain you!!

## My Make-Up
## (The Beauty Within)

My foundation are the values & morals
that I am covered with.

My shadow depicts my delicate lids that shuts ever so softly
as I pray in peace.

The mascara portrays bold visions that I see before me;
and allows insight of my past, present and future.

My blush is the happiness that exudes uncontrollably
with all that is good.

My lipstick illustrates the voice that validates my thoughts
with love, sincerity, validity & hope.

## CHAPTER ELEVEN
### Fighting For My Faith

The year 2020 was indeed a time of reflection, trying mental deliberation, bitter-sweet experiences and yes…a fight for my faith. During the beginning of the year the world was introduced and invaded by the Covid-19 pandemic. In many of our lives we had never experienced such an uncertain time. The world was shut down from travel, work, school, and everyday life luxuries that we took full advantage of, up until then.

In February 2020, I had all the symptoms of Covid but when I went to the emergency room via ambulance, and diagnosed, I was told that I only had flu symptoms and to take Tylenol with rest. The emergency room halls were filled with other patients with the same symptoms, and I heard too many patients told the same thing that was told to me. Covid was so new and mysterious. Thank God, I got past the excruciating pain, feeling of being underwater as I breathed, and being so weak. My children helped to care for both me and Cameron until I started to feel better.

In early March, Cameron was not feeling well so Imani took him to the emergency room at Children's Hospital. I was still recovering from feeling ill and didn't want to take any risk, so she demanded that I allow her to be the big sister and let her take the lead on making sure he got the care he needed. I was so thankful to her.  Afterall, she knew everything about him, and cared for him daily as his home care aid.  Once they arrived at the hospital, he was immediately admitted to the intensive care unit; and diagnosed with pneumonia.  In addition, he had suffered congestive heart failure, a collapsed lung, and an old wound that caused an infection throughout his body.  He also had to be put on a respirator to help him breath.  I spoke with the doctors and nurses everyday via phone calls while his siblings visited and checked on him daily.

I felt better a couple days later.  So, I took over.  By that time, the pandemic had really gotten bad, so the hospital began strict visiting limitations.  Soon, I was the only one that Cameron could have by his bed side daily.  Thank God, everything had shut down, so I didn't have to worry about work.  Instead, I was able to fully concentrate on being there for my baby boy.

I must say, it was very different seeing the hospital looking almost deserted and so quiet.  There was no free will of walking around or visitors entering the lobby constantly.  Patients and loved ones would have to stay in their room for the most part.  One cool aspect was that all patients had their own room with no roommate.  This gave a lot more space to move around within the room.  But it also became lonesome because when you got to meet a roommate and their family, it was as if they were your support during the stay.  Cameron had been hospitalized so much, that this was how we were used to things being done.  But again, Covid changed all of that.

As the weeks passed, I began to feel melancholy.  I knew that between not having that contact with family who would usually visit & relieve me during Cameron's admission; in addition to Cameron still not feeling well, I began to feel overwhelmed. As always, I knew that prayer would help. However, I must admit even that became very challenging. There were so many uncertainties that was thrust upon me instantaneously. The cardiologist was very worried that Cam would not recover from all that his body was going through this time. His heart was barely pumping so he had to be put on heart monitors to assist. The next few days were crucial to his survival. Usually, I knew how to stay focused, in control, and how to update the family without them feeling even more afraid of Cameron's prognosis. This time, it was not the case.

I went home to take a shower and return to the hospital as I did routinely. I cried all the way home and tried to think positive. As soon as I opened the door to my apartment, I felt like something snatched all the strength out of my body as I started to drop to my knees and cry uncontrollably. There was no if, ands, or buts about it…I was terrified for my son's life. I was so hurt emotionally that I pleaded and begged God to help me as I fight for my faith. I think that has got to be one of the hardest feelings that one can bear. When you believe in your spiritual upbringing and know that the devil is so busy that he can make you second guess the faith that has sustained you all your life. I cried, screamed and prayed as if I was in Sunday service at the pulpit.

There was no way that I could go back to that hospital with such a painful feeling to endure. So, I did what I was always taught to do. When you can't find the strength to pray for yourself, call someone who can do it with you. I called my children's godmother, Vicki. When she heard my plea for help over the phone, she immediately started praying as she cried with me. She could seemingly feel the hurt that I was going through because I had never done this before. I can't even tell you how long she stayed on the phone with me while praying as if her life depended on it. But I do recall eventually feeling a calmness as I began to wipe away the last bit of tears that I had left in my body and soul. I thank God for her in that instance, and as always. She truly helped me fight that battle with thy rod and thy staph. The resurgence of my faith had been renewed.

## CHAPTER TWELVE
### He Marches On

Cameron eventually recovered from his hospitalization and made a huge change. He gained weight which made him stronger, grew taller, and seemed to be the happiest ever. His facial features even changed. He had finally begun to look like a young man instead of his usual baby face. I was so excited about his weight gain. So much so, that I happily went on a shopping spree to buy him new clothes because he had finally outgrown his kid size clothes. I was so thrilled to be shopping in the young men section instead of the kids' department. I was up and down the isles like I owned the place and felt damn good doing it! The prices were in the budget which was always a plus. Mama always taught me to shop smart. She would have been proud of me that day because I made sure that her Cam-Cam, as she used to call him, was good with his new gear and my purse wasn't bare.

Again, with Covid-19 being in the midst, it allowed me the opportunity to work from home which was a blessing because I got to be with Cameron every day without being separated by him going to school and me working. He participated with virtual school, as best as he was able. His teacher Mrs. Hicks was great because she also made activity boxes for Cameron to work with as much as he would tolerate.  This also allowed him to not digress with what he had learned.  We would meet virtually for her to check on Cameron and go over updates.  She was truly a great support!

      On January 5, 2021, Cameron turned twenty years old!  Oh my God!! The thought took me back to when the doctors gave him only six months to live.  My heart rejoiced with feeling so blessed.  We celebrated his birthday with family, food, cake and laughs.  Cam was so happy when we sang at least three versions of Happy Birthday!  There was the traditional version, Stevie Wonder's version, and 50 Cent's version, "Go shorty, it's your birthday"!  Monai, hilariously, started rapping a few free style bars.  It was so funny because she didn't know what to say but she made it work as we all hyped her up!  Cameron laughed and enjoyed all that was going on around him.  And for a change, he didn't fall asleep during his birthday party!!

## CHAPTER THIRTEEN
### Doing Things Cam's Way

For some that knew Cameron, they had the privilege of seeing him grow and become such a resilient young man. From the moment I brought him home from the hospital, after he was born, I made up in my mind that he would be nurtured with pride; and taught to not give up. I am so thankful that having that mentality for the last twenty years has helped Cameron with becoming his own man, and one who has shown how to accomplish despite the medical challenges that he was living with.

Cameron lived a full quality of life done his way! He loved to hang out with the family by just being in the midst of what ever come what may. Music was one of his most enjoyable listening hobbies, ever since he was maybe two or three years of age. We noticed that when we played music, that he would immediately light up with smiles. One day, when he had the ability to utilize his stander, Monai decided to play some jams. T-Pain's "I'm In Love with a Stripper" blasted on the speaker. Don't you know, Cameron's arms went up as far as he could get them, and he began to bounce with smiles & nods of enjoyment! We laughed so hard and was simply amazed!! He did his thing to the beat. He looked like he was having such a good time that we joined him. We took every opportunity to make him feel like he was a apart of all we did!

## Unbeknownst To Me

One of the biggest highlights that I can recall is when Cameron went to senior prom. My son Taji and I accompanied him to the hall, and I felt like I was the happiest mama ever. The family came over as we got dressed and took so many photos. I rented a SUV so that we could have enough room for his wheelchair and just because all of my other children had rentals as well. Again, Cameron was not going to be excluded from anything if it was in my power. Anyway, as we drove off the block, it was full of on lookers with music blasting. Imani & Monai had a special song that they played from their car as they literally followed us to the freeway with celebratory cheers, yells and honking horns! They had Mack Avenue drivers so hyped that suddenly, we began to hear horns and congrats from all types of folks. It was simply an amazing feeling!

Once we arrived at the venue where prom was being held, Taji took over. He had Cameron all over that ballroom! One minute I'd see them next to me; the next on the dance floor; then taking pictures or on live video! I could tell that it was an extra proud moment for Taji with him being able to share that special day with his baby brother. We all enjoyed ourselves…especially Cameron.

On high school graduation day, Chene Park (now referred to as The Aretha) was full of Diane Banks-Williamson (DBW) and East English Preparatory High school graduates and families. I pushed Cameron in his wheelchair to his position on stage so that he would be ready to receive his diploma once his name was called. I made my way back to my family to take my seat and got ready to see my baby be celebrated! Cameron's school was the smaller of the two schools. So, with all of our student's families we took up only about three full rows. As the names began to get called, I felt myself getting more and more excited. Then, his name was announced…Cameron Sheppard! It felt like the whole amphitheater lit up with cheers & standing ovations as my baby was pushed to the podium to get his diploma! Tears of happiness poured from my eyes as I thanked God for making all of this happen. After the ceremony, the family went to dinner to celebrate yet another milestone and victory that Cameron had accomplished.

    I made sure that Cameron was included in as much as possible. After all, that played a big part with helping with his social skills & emotional stability. We went on road trips, family functions, parks, & school trips just to name a few. On occasion, I would randomly do pop-up visits at his schools (elementary, middle, high & transitional) just to make sure that he was being treated with inclusion. I am proud to say that the staff always made sure that he was. He was even quite the "Ladies Man". He had many cuties that made sure they gave him attention while at school.

    So, as you can see, Cameron lived his life, and we made the necessary adjustments as needed. I wasn't one for pushing him to do what he didn't feel like doing. But I certainly made sure that he did not feel excluded. It was always important for us to pay attention to his mood and expressions because he could not verbalize his feelings. By doing so, we learned what his likes and dislikes were. It also forced us to not give up on his happiness by putting limitations on his abilities and decisions. As the saying goes "Don't ever dis…his ability"! In other words, dismissing his abilities would not be tolerated and used as an excuse to not support Cameron. And just as anyone else, he has a right to practice the autotomy that the good Lord had given him. So what, if we had to make the adjustment. It was the fact that he could express himself to the degree of self-gratification and expression. I was determined not allow anyone to deny him his own source of power.

### Find Your Destination

Your here is not your destination.
It's just the beginning.

Being here is only a pathway to get to your ultimate goal of arriving to your destination.

There are hard roads,
as well as easy ones

Which way are you willing to go,
to find the beauty to your destination?

## CHAPTER FOURTEEN
Heaven Awaits

On February 28, 2021, I woke up that morning to start our daily routine of going to Cameron's room to say good morning, prepare his medication and tube feed. He would usually respond immediately as if waiting for me to greet him. Cameron always woke up super early in the morning and would always either turn his head towards my voice or give a morning laugh. As I walked over to his bed, I noticed that his ear was a little pale. I then felt his shoulder that was chilly. I thought nothing of it; and told him "Aww Cam, you must have gotten a little chilly last night from this dehumidifier". Then I proceeded to warm him up by rubbing his shoulder. Still no response. I suddenly stood still and shook him a little not to startle him, as I thought he was sleeping. Still no response. I then tried to reposition him. Still no response. Then I stared at his peaceful face and asked God if this is what I thought it was. As I then gently leaned over to embrace him, I held him firmly to find that his body was still warm. A silent moment of peace came over me.

Sure enough, no breaths, no movement. I immediately tried to give CPR and called 911. As the 911 operator tried to comfort and direct me on compressions, my heart felt weaker and weaker with each push. But I stayed focused. It was if God had me in his hand and had all control. As the paramedics rushed to Cameron's bedroom, they worked hard to bring him back. By this time my son Taji arrived…but too late. He could only break down in tears and rush to his baby brother's side as he always did. I will never forget the way he straddled his whole body and just held Cameron with the tenderness that he always held him with. Then came Imani who was so hurt she cried with rage. I had to hold her as we wrestled in the middle of the floor while she asked…why, why my baby brother? Monai was also so torn and hurt. She could only hug us & cry. Cameron's father and the rest of the family urgently came in one by one. We each gave Cameron our last hugs and kisses before he was prepped to be taken out of our home. We all held one another and escorted him outside; watched the medical examiner's van take my baby away, and disappear, as they turned the corner.

## CHAPTER FIFTEEN
### Manifested with Love

As I later began to think about how things went that morning, I came to realize that Cameron completed his mission of teaching us love, strength, and happiness. God gave him to me unexpectedly with peace, and took him back to heaven, with peace. He even allowed me to sleep and wake with no interruption. As if preparing me for the task at hand. In other words, things could have been a lot worse, but it wasn't. God couldn't have done it any better way.

I always asked God to never put me in a position to have to decide to take Cameron off of life support; if he ever passed away that he was not alone or being hurt; and for him to be home with his family without pain. God gave me that and more. Don't get me wrong, I miss hugging him, laughing with him, looking at tv and listening to music, going on family outings, visiting him at school and all the other things that made him happy. But I feel that he is still laughing in heaven and is truly at peace because of the love we gave him. Which was a result of the reciprocated love he innocently gave to us.

Although Cameron had many medical issues, he was a happy, courageous, loving, inspirational, resilient and persistent young man. Many people used the word struggle when describing his life, but if you ask me and those who were with him constantly, we will say brave.

Cameron has left a legacy with us. So many people knew him, and he touched their lives in so many positive ways. I'm talking folks from all walks of life: young, old, professionals, even homeboys in the neighborhood who took the time to say hi to Cameron and seemingly be at peace with themselves if only for a minute. My son was an amazing young man. I've witnessed many changes for the good of others while he was on this earth, and since he has passed. He was truly a genuine jewel. The hearts and souls that he has touched will never be forgotten from those that got to experience his silent greatness.

## CHAPTER SIXTEEN
Reflection

As I sit here rejoicing about Cameron, I am praising God for continuing to get me through the heartache with mercy and grace. Not to long ago, I got in my car and went for a ride. I began to feel a certain kind of way from acknowledging that complete closure from Cameron's passing away was evident and in the midst. I must admit that each time I contacted different agencies and or supports that helped Cameron, to notify them of his death, it forced me to let go of some of my guard in order to grieve a little bit more. After all, I would not be able to advocate for him anymore which was difficult for me to accept. I changed his diapers, fed him, laughed and cried with him, made all of his decisions, spoke for him, and made sure I put my all into making sure he was well taken care of.

I did everything for him for two whole decades. To give a better perspective…if you break that down further, that's 7,300 days; 175,200 hours; or 10,512,000 minutes. That's a long time.

It hurts that I will no longer have such an important responsibility anymore. I'm not quite sure if I am being selfish with my thoughts. But at this point, I feel it is ok for me to feel what I feel. However, taking the time I need for full closer helps me with knowing that I did my best and didn't fail him. I thank God that I am allowed to question my thoughts and be ok with doing so. Peace is what I continuously work towards, and I know that my days wont always be easy. But I am thankful that peace is said to be everlasting, so there is no rush. I have plenty of time to work it out! The reconciliation and tranquility that I hold on too is my ultimate truth.

## CHAPTER SEVENTEEN
### Commissioned by Cameron

Having Cameron in my life has taught me so many things. Most of all, the heart is the life of all that it is attached with. Cam enriched me with the ability to live for myself, as well as for him. He influenced me to elevate the potential that was dormant inside of me. After all, I had no choice but to walk in a life of persistence and resiliency. For if I didn't, who knows what type of life I would have led for me or my children.

The heart represents love. We all need love, compassion, and touch. I can recall plenty of days when we would simply go give Cameron a hug just to feel better ourselves. Those hugs made us feel like we were getting so much love back. He had the warmest touch and would make this soothing sound as if he was saying "thanks and I love you too". It was such an endearing feeling!

Along with that came the ability to forgive. I had to hold true to that process with the ones that hurt me. For instance, my ex-husband. Although we went through so many struggles, I had to forgive him in order to find the peace that I needed to move on. I got my power back that way; and have been a better person because of it. We get along fine now and have respect for the friendship that remains. No one ever said to forget…it's the forgiveness that is the key!

*My journey continues!!*

## Unbeknownst to Me

Cameron...My Baby,
Unbeknownst to me...when God placed you in my womb, he had a special plan. You entered my life when I needed you the most. As you continued to grow inside of me, we bonded in a special way. And from that moment, we remained as one.

Unbeknownst to me...God set a purpose for you as he created you in life form. You see, I recognized that everything about you was angelic. Your ultrasound even showed a halo crowning your head.

Unbeknownst to me...Your purpose would prove time and time again that your mission was to bring love, peace, and happiness to everyone who crossed your path. It didn't matter if they met you once, or many times. You showed how to conquer despite the challenge; persist with humility & grace; and value a pure heart & loyalty. You gave me encouragement, a voice, empowerment, strength, inspiration and dedication.

Unbeknownst to me...while I cared for you, I learned to care for myself; while I loved you, I learned to love myself; while I prayed for you, I learned to pray for myself; while I made sure you had a smile, I even had one for myself. You were sent to me for a reason and this I know to be true...

Thank you, My Baby for giving me life (joy), a reason to exist (advocate), and for showing me how to purposely walk tall, with an even stride (pride). For if it had not been for you, I wouldn't be me. I owe you for all the greatness that you have bestowed upon me. I thank you my baby, for being my son, my friend, & my spiritual guide. I thank God for you and will see you again!

May your smiles make the angels themselves rejoice!! Well done my baby...well done!

Weeping may endure for a night;
but joy cometh in the morning.

-Psalm 30:5

# CONTACT INFORMATION

Correspondence can be sent via email

to

# Marlo Sheppard

ms.unbeknownst@gmail.com

Cover, Set Up, Formatting, Editing & Publishing Assistance by

## Phillip "UcciKhan" Sample

## For Free Consultation

uccikhan@yahoo.com

Unbeknownst To Me

Made in the USA
Monee, IL
18 May 2025